AVAILABLE
(805)948-0721

**Does
Advertising
Tell the
Truth?**

Advertising

AVAILABLE
(805)948-0721
CALIFORNIA CITY
LAKESHORE INN
TEHACHAPI EXIT

DEBATING
THE ISSUES

Does Advertising Tell the Truth?

Advertising

**AUBREY
HICKS**

Cavendish
Square

New York

Published in 2014 by Cavendish Square Publishing, LLC
303 Park Avenue South, Suite 1247, New York, NY 10010

Library of Congress Cataloging-in-Publication Data

Hicks, Aubrey.
Advertising : does advertising tell the truth? / Aubrey Hicks.
  pages cm. — (Debating the issues)
Includes index.
ISBN 978-1-62712-404-1 (hardcover) ISBN 978-1-62712-405-8 (paperback)
ISBN 978-1-62712-406-5 (ebook)
1. Deceptive advertising—Juvenile literature. 2. Advertising—Moral and ethical aspects—Juvenile literature. I. Title.
HF5827.8.H53 2014
659.1—dc23
2013031806

Editor: Peter Mavrikis
Art Director: Anahid Hamparian
Series design by Sonia Chaghatzbanian
Production Manager: Jennifer Ryder-Talbot
Production Editor: Andrew Coddington

Photo research by Alison Morretta

Printed in the United States of America

Table of Contents

Chapter 1

Unless you happen to be standing in the middle of the woods, in handmade clothes, using only tools you made from the rocks and sticks in the area, you can probably look around you and see advertisements (often shortened to ads) of many kinds.

What Is Advertising?

Advertisements are messages that persuade an audience to change **ideals** or behavior in some way. We usually think of ads as the way a company communicates with consumers in order to generate sales. From the large **billboards** seen on buses or buildings to tiny **logos** on sneakers and the **banners** on web pages, ads surround us. The following are just a few of the forms ads can come in:

Posters	Newspapers
Brochures	Television commercials
Paintings	Online pop-ups and banners
Billboards	on receipts or tickets
Postcards	Pens
Stickers	Product logos
Magazines	Media product placement

Ads surround us. Times Square in New York City is filled with ads, from company names high atop the skyscrapers, to signs and posters closer to eye level, to logos on cars and people's clothing.

Seen here on the foot of a soccer player in Manchester, England, the Nike® Swoosh is an internationally recognized logo.

The full list of all the different kinds of advertisements is much longer. All of these various kinds of ads exist because there are many different reasons for placing an ad. The type of communication, or **medium**, changes as the **target** of the ad changes. For example, kids selling lemonade in their neighborhood on a Saturday don't need to put commercials on television stations. A sign to let people driving or walking by the lemonade stand know the price is enough to reach the intended audience. However, if those kids wanted to bottle that lemonade and sell it in grocery stores, then some kind of advertising to spread the news about the new lemonade would be needed.

A Brief History of Advertising

While advertising has been around for as long as civilizations were trading goods with each other, the advertising industry is a relatively new business. Most historians agree that advertising as an industry took root in the mid–1800s. One hundred and fifty years ago, a person wanting to buy soap would have bought it at a local market from the person who made it. The technological advances of the **Industrial Revolution** made it possible to produce more things faster and ship them anywhere in the world. Fast-forwarding through history, a person today is able to choose from hundreds of different stores with thousands of different brands.

Selling wares to neighbors didn't require much planning or **marketing**. Once manufacturers could sell to people anywhere in the world, they had to find a way to make customers want their product more than that of a competitor. How did a company make its product stand out from similar local products? Manufacturers started by placing short notices in newspapers. A company would purchase the space in the newspaper from an adman, who received a **commission** for his services. The newspaper didn't write the text that was used in the ads.

Instead, the information came from the company buying the space in the paper. By the mid–1800s, a handful of enterprising admen started a new business: the advertising agency. These agencies quickly grew into a complex industry.

Many of the early admen left the newspapers and became **copywriters** at ad agencies. The copywriter's job was to come up with the text of the ads and other materials for **publicity**. Copywriters would carefully pick the right words to promote the product with the goal of getting the most people they could to purchase it. As more and more companies turned to advertising agencies to get a leg up on their competition, the advertisers realized they needed to learn more about the science of the advertisement. They asked themselves what made one product sell more than another.

In the late 1800s advertisers started creating illustrated characters to convey meaningful ideals or stories for the **brands**. One of the first popular characters in an ad was the Arrow Collar Man, created by a famous illustrator named Joseph C. Leyendecker for the agency N. W. Ayer and Son. The Arrow Collar Man was not a real person but a set of characters created to give **consumers** the idea of what kind of man wore the company's shirts and detachable collars. This character ran in advertisements from 1905 through 1931. He was suave and sophisticated, good-looking and carefree, and just as comfortable and fashionable at home reading the newspaper as he was out on a date with a beautiful woman. The character reflected the ideals and **mores** of the time period, and people who saw the ads in

This little girl is drawn to the cute characters on this 1930s billboard. What do you think this ad is selling?

newspapers and magazines loved the ideals the Arrow Collar Man represented. Illustration and text went together to create a world in which this man could live and breathe in the imaginations of the people who saw the ads. Sales of the shirts increased, and customers even wrote fan mail to the "white-collar men," though they were only painted characters.

The Arrow Collar Man and Nipper, the dog pictured staring into the horn of a **gramophone** and listening to his owner's voice, became synonymous with the brands they served. These images were identified with these brands for many years.

Volney B. Palmer opened the first American advertising agency in 1842 in Philadelphia, Pennsylvania. Fewer than ten agencies operated worldwide during the second half of the 1800s. During this time, these agencies studied the power of advertising. The English historian Thomas B. Macaulay said, "Nothing except the mint can make money without advertising." Advertisers, who quickly learned this bit of commercial wisdom, found new ways of creating advertising campaigns designed to make the most money for themselves and their clients. Experimentation with the power of **branding** focused on

DID YOU KNOW?

One of advertising's first sales tactics was the creation of fictional characters associated with the brand. Such products as M&M's® and Mr. Clean® still employ this strategy successfully.

NIPPER AND CHIPPER

A painting called *His Master's Voice*, by Francis Barraud, was bought and trademarked by the Victor Talking Machine Company. The painting showed a dog named Nipper, a Jack Russell terrier, listening to a gramophone with his head cocked in recognition of his master's voice coming through the machine. When Victor trademarked this painting in 1899, Nipper became associated with the company, and it lasted through its many changes in ownership and technology for more than ninety years. It is considered one of the most successful advertising strategies of the twentieth century. Commercials as late as the 1990s featured a Jack Russell named Nipper and a puppy named Chipper that interacted with the television the same way the original Nipper did with that first gramophone.

Nipper was a widely recognized symbol of sound quality for decades.

The U.S. Treasury created the war savings stamp program to raise money for World War I and World War II. The campaign, as you see here, was targeted to school-age children.

ads on public transportation and in brochures and catalogs. The industry grew and changed so much during the latter half of the 1800s and the beginning of the 1900s that the government turned to admen during World War I. Advertisers were able to use the power of branding to get the American people behind the war movement.

Who Are Advertisers?

Advertising is a powerful and complex industry. There are many people involved in the process. An ad begins with the **client**, the company that is selling a product or service. Let's take an imaginary product through the process of advertising. Let's say the client wants to take the lemonade previously sold only in the neighborhood and sell it nationwide in grocery stores, convenience stores, and even online. Let's call the company Fresh Lemons.

As the client, Fresh Lemons starts by selecting an advertising agency. Today there are many agencies to choose from. The top moneymakers in the country include Omnicom Group, WPP Group, and Inter-

> ## DID YOU KNOW?
> There are different kinds of ad agencies. General agencies do everything for the client. Media agencies focus on buying ad placements. There are also specialized agencies. One company might do advertising only for the medical industry. Another agency might only focus on want ads. Some large manufacturers even set up their own in-house ad agency, a department within the company, rather than go to an outside agency.

public Group of Companies (IPG), to name a few. A client can also choose from one of the dozens of smaller agencies, depending on the company's needs. Once an agency is chosen, the client is assigned to an account executive, who will make sure the whole process works smoothly. The account executive works with the different departments and also works with outside companies, such as printers, to keep the client aware of each part of the process.

Once the client meets with the agency representatives, the researchers, and the creative directors, the advertising agency develops a marketing plan. If the client likes the direction of the plan, the production departments create the artwork or websites needed to sell the product. Media planners purchase time and space to place the ads on TV shows, in magazines, online, and more. Depending on the type of **campaign**, ads are sometimes sent to survey companies to test the strength or popularity of the ads.

The final people involved in the advertising process are the consumers. Consumers see the ads on their way to work, hear them on the radio, see them on television, on the Internet, and in magazines and newspapers. If the advertiser has done a good job, the ad and the product will be memorable. The next time the consumer needs or wants that kind of product, he or she will remember the ad and purchase it from the client.

If the advertiser has done an excellent job, consumers will purchase the product or service even though they never wanted or needed it

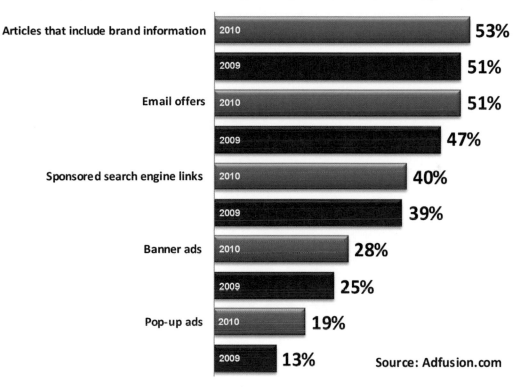

Consumer Likelihood to Read and Act Upon Online Advertising Tactics

Articles that include brand information	2010	53%
	2009	51%
Email offers	2010	51%
	2009	47%
Sponsored search engine links	2010	40%
	2009	39%
Banner ads	2010	28%
	2009	25%
Pop-up ads	2010	19%
	2009	13%

Source: Adfusion.com

Opinion Research Corporation survey of 1,053 Americans 18 and older conducted March 2010. Chart shows respondents indicating they are "very likely" or "somewhat likely" to read and act upon each type of ad.

before they saw the ad. If the agency is successful with the ad campaign for Fresh Lemons, the result will be a demand for the lemonade from both retail stores and the consumer.

These are just a few of the kinds of people involved in ad creation and distribution. Other people that are part of the process in some

TRADEMARK SYMBOLS

The symbol for a registered trademark, a circled R (usually appearing as the symbol ®) is used to indicate that a particular word, phrase, or logo has been legally associated with a specific product or service. A trademark symbol protects the company from others taking the name, phrase, or logo for their own use. For example, there is only one company that can call its candy-coated chocolates M&Ms® since the name is protected under a registered trademark. The other symbols used to claim ownership are the ™ and ℠. The TM mark indicates that the brand or product associated with it is not registered. The same is true for the SM mark, which is used to label services.

Recognized all over the world, the Coca-Cola® bottle is almost as widely known as the registered trademark logo.

way or another include **psychologists**, **economists**, doctors, and representatives from many other professions. The psychologist's task is to research and determine how people react to ads in order to create ads that target specific audiences. Economists working at big financial firms use advertising to make decisions about which companies to invest in. Doctors use marketing materials from pharmaceutical companies to make decisions about which drugs to prescribe to patients. Without the consumer, the company could not sell the product or service. Therefore, the consumer is the key person considered in ad creation and distribution.

Is Advertising Beneficial to Society?

Organizations in the United States spend over $300 billion a year on advertising. Ads create controversy. They are regulated by the government to protect consumers from being persuaded with falsehoods. Ads are scrutinized by consumers, manufacturers, the government, and academics. They can be funny or serious or almost invisible. Ads surround us in many forms, including T-shirt logos, banners on apps, book covers, and television commercials. In 1997 the Vatican's Pontifical Council stated, "Just as the media of social communication themselves have enormous influence everywhere, so advertising, using media as its vehicle, is a pervasive, powerful force shaping attitudes and behavior in today's world." An administrative department of the Catholic Church used this statement to begin a long document offering guidelines about the nature and appropriate uses of advertising.

If every organization and company takes part in some sort of advertising, how do we determine whether advertising is beneficial to society? To answer that question properly, one must first determine whether the goods or services are beneficial to society. Just as the old saying, "The ends don't justify the means" reminds us, it isn't necessarily true that advertising is beneficial just because the products or services that are sold or traded are beneficial.

One must consider the effects on the individual, on society, and on the world in addition to the effects on the companies and organizations that provide all the goods and services. Perhaps looking at some positive and negative effects of advertising will help you reach a decision.

WHAT DO YOU THINK?

Do you notice advertisements other than commercials on television? Take a look around the room you are in; how many marketing tools do you see? What do these ads mean to you? How do they make you feel?

Are there commercials you like? What are they, and do they make you want to buy the product?

Have you talked about advertising with your family or teachers? If you have, what did they say about it?

A marketing professional named Jason Love once said, "So long as there's a jingle in your head, television isn't free." What do you think he meant?

Has advertising ever had a noticeable effect on you or someone close to you?

Chapter 2

In so many ways advertising is integral to our economy and our way of life. The industry itself is a $300–billion business. There are millions of people who work in the advertising industry. Some people work specifically in advertising agencies, while others are indirectly involved through manufacturers, health care organizations, or nonprofit companies. Advertising attempts to bring consumers together with the goods and services they need or want. The British statesman Winston Churchill said, "Advertising nourishes the consuming power of men. It creates want for a better standard of living. It spurs individual exertion and greater production." In the competitive marketplace, entrepreneurs and companies need creative advertising of their goods or services in order to capture consumer loyalty. Studying the popularity of advertising trends tells historians much about the culture of the time. Advertising is youthful and reflects popular culture. Advertising that allows people to connect with each other through cultural references generates conversation and communication.

The Want Ad

The earliest and simplest type of advertisement is the **classified ad**, often called the want ad. Simply stated, it is a short text ad that lists

The first newspaper classified ad was published in 1631. Newspapers still print classified ads today. Want ads are one of the cheapest and easiest ways to connect goods or services with consumers.

goods or services for sale or goods and services needed. Employment postings are want ads; the employer buys the ad space to declare that there is a position open. People place want ads every day. It is one of the quickest and easiest ways for consumers to connect with the goods or services they need.

Almost four hundred years ago Theophraste Renaudot, a French doctor, started a notice board for employers and job seekers. It grew so popular as people began posting all sorts of want ads that he started the first newspaper (*La Gazette*). In 1631, the newspaper was invented to meet a need people had to communicate and connect for the sole purpose of exchanging goods or services. It began by printing classifieds. Popularity for this sort of notice board has never stopped. In the early twenty-first century many people use the Internet for this purpose. For example, a popular classified service, craigslist, became the first stop for many people looking for a new apartment, a new or used bike, or even a job. The simple want ad is a necessity for people looking to exchange services or goods.

As modern society turns toward ways to be eco-friendly, the simple want ad allows people to recycle or up-cycle rather than throw away used items. Without the want ad, it would be hard to sell a used refrigerator or microwave. Publishing a want ad is a way of letting people know that an item is available.

Classified ads are still one of the first things people turn to when looking for employment. Companies and organizations post want ads for open positions on their own websites, in magazines, with online

People look to craigslist, a free online site, to post want ads. Have stuff to sell? Need someone to mow your lawn? Looking for a job? Need an apartment? Look no further than your desktop, laptop, or smartphone.

job-search engines, and in local and national newspapers. Think how hard it would be if every person looking for a job had to go door-to-door just to see whether a company had an opening. There are even large companies that exist solely to fill job openings with people whose skills match an employer's needs.

With Competition Comes Creativity

Before mass production of goods, people bought or traded for items from people they knew and trusted. As soon as **cottage industries** became factories and items were mass-produced, manufacturers had to find ways to make their products stand out. One of the more important parts of advertising is branding. Branding creates a story for a company or service that helps convince the consumer to trust and like the product.

As early as the late 1880s, about forty years after the first ad agency, advertisers discovered the power of the **endorsement**. One of the first branding successes came to Pears Soap. Soap was a product that for hundreds of years had been made in the household or bought from local

merchants for the sole purpose of cleaning. In 1888 Pears Soap featured an ad using a quotation from the beautiful British actress Lillie Langtry in newspapers in England and the United States. The ad, accompanied by an image and the signature of the actress, read, "For the hands and complexion I prefer it to any other." Pears Soap became branded as the "famous English complexion soap." The goal was to make everyday people want to use the same soap that kept the famous and beautiful actress looking good.

This ad from the late 1880s has all the manufacturer's claims written directly on the ad space. Today advertisers tend to use a more subtle and sophisticated form of getting their point across to consumers.

Other soap manufacturers competing with Pears didn't have a celebrity endorsement. They experimented with scents, ingredients, and packaging. One company even created a "celebrity." The Gibson Girl, an image promoted as an ideal for the American woman, was used to sell No. 4711 White Rose Glycerine Soap. The accompanying text described White Rose Glycerine soap as "transparent as crystal, fragrant as flowers" and claimed that the soap could "be applied to the most tender and delicate skin." Cosmetics and soap manufacturers soon began using the science of chemistry to create new and different products that would be better for the skin, last longer in the pantry, and leave a longer-lasting scent on the skin. In 1957 the Dove® beauty bar was created and promoted as the one cleanser that wouldn't dry the skin.

Dove remains a top-selling soap brand today, with faithful users even in a very competitive market with hundreds of different brands vying for customer loyalty. In 2004 Dove started a "campaign for real beauty" to

DID YOU KNOW?

The Gibson Girl, who existed only on the printed page, was a promotional idealization of how advertisers believed many women saw themselves or desired others to see them. The image, created by the artist Charles Dana Gibson, was very successful for the manufacturers and advertisers of the product it promoted.

COMPANY SLOGANS

The key in many marketing plans is something called a **slogan**. Slogans are also known in the United States as taglines. A slogan is a motto or a phrase used in a marketing campaign that represents the central idea behind the campaign. Some slogans stand the test of time. For example, Maxwell House coffee has used the tagline "Good to the last drop" since 1907. Companies sometimes change a slogan to better represent the brand or to reach new audiences. The fast-food chain McDonald's has changed its slogan several times. Here are some examples: "We love to see you smile," "McDonald's. I'm loving it," and "What we're made of."

Do you recognize the Maxwell House slogan from commercials?

further distinguish the brand name from its competitors. The campaign was designed to have the soap's users discuss the definition of beauty and what beauty means in real life versus the artificial beauty seen in the advertising of the other major brands.

British politician John Enoch Powell described advertising as freedom:

"Remove advertising, disable a person or firm from proclaiming its wares and their merits, and the whole of society and of the economy is transformed. The enemies of advertising are the enemies of freedom."

Technology allowed manufacturers to expand out of the house and neighborhood and into a worldwide market. Advertising helped to create that worldwide market and continues to keep manufacturers striving to make newer and better products. Without the competition there would never have been any need to make the product better. Once a company makes a best-selling product, it still must continue to be creative with the product or service as well as with its advertising in order to remain a competitor.

Competition among major manufacturers in many different industries has led to major advancements. The introductions of the iPod and iTunes in 2001 by the Apple corporation led to a huge surge in the portable music industry. Some would argue that iTunes also created a revolution in how music is bought and sold and how people find out about musicians new to them. The popularity and demand for this type of product created a huge shift in the computer and cell phone

REAL VERSUS IDEAL BEAUTY

Some companies use many different tactics to try to get people to buy products. Dove has several campaigns that seem to contradict one another. The brand ideal for the skin care line is of "real beauty." When Dove says "real" it means real compared to the airbrushed falseness of the beauty industry in general. The ideal that Dove is trying to sell in its ads is that everyone is beautiful, even those who are different from the perfect ideals of Hollywood. Dove is selling the idea that we should embrace wrinkles, freckles, an average weight, and other things that are usually airbrushed away in other commercials.

industries. In 2001 the original iPod had a storage capability of 5 or 10 gigabytes (GB), weighed 6.5 ounces, had no photo or video capability, could connect only to another device using firewire, and took three hours to fully charge the battery, which had a life of ten hours. By the fifth generation, released in 2012, the iPod Touch had increased storage (people could choose between 8, 32, and 64 GB), weighed 3.1 ounces, had photo and video playing capability, could connect to the Internet wirelessly, and could fully charge in four hours for a forty-hour music play or eight-hour video play. Steve Jobs, Apple's founder who led the company during this growth period, was known for inspiring creativity and forward-thinking. He once said, "Being the richest man in the cemetery doesn't matter to me…Going to bed at night saying we've done something wonderful, that's what matters to me." Innovation was what mattered, and Apple strove to enter new markets by concentrating on "the things that are really important."

You have to wonder whether Apple would have worked so hard to create something new and different if there hadn't been another huge computer firm competing for customer loyalty. The Microsoft and Apple rivalry created an innovative and dynamic industry that revolutionized the way the world communicated, worked, and played.

Between 2001 and 2013 "smartphones" went from being owned by a few elites in business to being over 70 percent of the mobile phone market. In 2001 most cell phones could call, text, and take photos. By 2013 most cell phones could connect to the Internet, call, text

To this woman walking down a street in New York City's NoHo neighborhood, ads for the iPod are part of the scenery.

message, take photos, record videos, play games, and download applications. The huge surge in mobile technology over the past decade is due to the extreme demand and competition in the industry. Each brand releases a new cutting-edge phone every few months in order to stay ahead of or in step with the competition.

Newer and better products are also why advertising is essential to society. Technology changes so quickly; without advertising, most of us would never realize how much is changing around us. We might not know there are better options. When buying a new phone, we might not be aware that there is another phone that is more energy efficient, has a longer-lasting battery, or has better features for staying connected to friends, family, and business associates.

Competition for customer loyalty drives manufacturers to develop newer and better products. Newer and better products create more demand and keep the economy moving forward. What Churchill said in the mid–1900s is even more relevant in today's speed-of-light media world. The dramatic shift in our connectivity created its own revolution

Recent developments have transformed the smartphone from something for business to something for everyone. Here, a student learns to write Japanese characters on an iPhone.

in the media. As a society we have created technology that allows us to go back to a cottage industry and still promote our goods or services to the whole world. Large corporations thrive in the competitive industry, and we now live in a world in which even small entrepreneurial businesses can compete and succeed amid the competition.

Reflection of Popular Culture

The goal of the ad is to reach as many people as possible, to connect with something in the consumers and make them want the product. Ads are about reaching the inner core of who we are as a society. Ads reflect society's basic desires and fears. As our societal ethics, fears, and beliefs change over time, advertisers change their tactics to reflect these changes. Ads thus become excellent historical documentation of societal changes.

Through print ads you can trace the growth of radio and then the growth of television. Before the invention of the television, radio was a dominant form of entertainment, and companies found many ways to sell their products using it. Companies created entertaining shows to go along with their product and encourage people to buy the product. In 1924 Betty Crocker® sponsored a radio program called "Kitchen-Tested," which aired three times a week, to share recipes using Gold Medal Flour with listeners. The show offered listeners the chance to mail in a reply card and a few cents for a recipe box with "kitchen-tested" recipes. The announcement ads for the radio show had a woman and microphone illustrated above the program description.

33

Before World War II most ads targeting women were about home life and focused on such things as cooking, cleaning, and taking care of the family. When Pearl Harbor was bombed and the United States was drawn into the conflict in Europe, manufacturers and advertisers worked with the government in aid of the war effort. Some advertising was aimed at reinforcing the new roles taken by women whose menfolk had been shipped overseas. The now famous image of Rosie the Riveter (1942) showed a woman in overalls with her sleeves rolled up and her muscle flexed. The words "We Can Do It!" accompanied the image. Rosie was targeted at young women who, had there not been a war, would probably have been starting a family. Instead, they were being asked to come out in droves to build tanks, planes, and weapons for the war effort.

When the war ended, the men returning from abroad needed jobs. Advertisers were used to bring women back into the home. The ads of the 1950s were awash with women back in dresses, no more overalls. Ads from just after World War II give a sense that America was trying to regain the time before the war. Along with a sense of nostalgia for a time past, there was also a sense of great change. New technology was being created at an amazing pace and an individual's connection to the outside world was more global than in any other time before. Cars, still a relatively new invention, were larger, faster, and cheaper and could take a family farther than ever before.

One of the most successful marketing campaigns began in 1954, when Philip Morris launched a new ad for Marlboro cigarettes. The

"Rosie the Riveter" became a powerful symbol of patriotic duty during World War II. Today the same image is used to promote women's issues.

"Marlboro Man" was born. He was a rugged, cowboy type, an all-American man. A myth was born, and an American ideal was created along with the Marlboro Man. Just as the Gibson Girl was the American everywoman of the early twentieth century, the Marlboro Man was the American everyman of the mid–1900s.

DID YOU KNOW?

Both Wayne McLaren and David McLean were models used for the Philip Morris Marlboro Man campaigns. Both had a smoking habit, and both died from lung cancer.

While the 1950s were about trying to go back to the way things were before the war changed everything, the 1960s and 1970s were about revolution and modernization and celebrated technological advancement. Advertisers recognized this shift. In reaction to the civil rights movement—and the emergence of the hippie and other youth subcultures—advertisers started repositioning their brands as ethical and down to earth. For example, Bell System ads such as "Reach out and touch someone" stressed that long-distance telephone calls could connect people to their loved ones. International Business Machines (IBM), founded in 1924, advertised its commitment to innovation and progress.

Looking at an ad from the past can help you think about the society and the culture it was aimed at. It can tell you a little bit about the technology of the time and about the people who lived during that time. After only a hundred or so years of advertisements, people saw the connection between a society and its ads. During the war the British author Norman Douglas famously said, "You can tell the ideals of a nation by its advertising."

What's My Tribe?

If ads from the past can tell us about the society of the time, what can ads of the present tell us? Advertisements have an amazing ability to make us want some things and not want other things. They help us figure ourselves out. Are you a Mac or a PC?

Psychologists and **anthropologists** study the concept of subculture. Each person has his or her own geographical culture. Are you American, English, Spanish or some other nationality? Is that all you are? Perhaps you also identify yourself with a more specific geographical range? Are you a city person or a rural person? Are you a New Yorker or an Iowan?

These identities help fit you into subcultures, or tribes, within the larger culture. Other things define who a person is within society: the music he or she listens to, the kinds of hobbies a person has, the kind of computer a person prefers, the kinds of clothes he or she wears. And does the person wear jewelry or have a tattoo? All of these things connect us to the other people who do or like the same things we do or like ourselves.

DID YOU KNOW?

Many tribes begin with an idea. For instance, the term *emo* originally was used to describe a style of music influenced by punk. It grew to a point where it described a whole subculture from musicians to fans, even a style of clothing. Today a person may be called emo even if he or she does not listen to the music that created the culture.

Advertising attempts to reach into the unconscious mind to find a way to make us want or think we need something. Ads provoke;

consumers may remember or forget an ad, love or hate it. As we grow up, our reactions to ads help us figure out where we fit into society. When we see a commercial, part of our brain is focused on the question "Am I the kind of person who likes this?" When we see a **trailer** for a movie, we aren't just watching to see what the movie is about, we are also determining how our preferences fit in with our peers'.

A trailer or ad for a horror film will provoke fear and hope. A story about a fictional monster is scary, but there is the hope that the characters seen in the trailer will outwit or outrun the monster, and even defeat it by the end of the movie. When a person sees the trailer, he or she has a reaction to the fear and hope the ad is designed to produce. Does this person like horror films? Monster movies? Are the actors in the film people this person admires? The answers to these questions lead to the decision to see or not to see the movie.

First we determine whether we identify with the brand and then how we identify with the brand, and finally we determine whether we like or dislike the brand. Buying clothes, for example, is about cost and style. It is also about fitting in with other people who are like us (or standing out from the crowd). The ads we see every day help us determine where we fit into society. Advertising also helps us define the people around us.

Of course, advertising isn't always about buying goods or services. Advertising is also about promoting action. Advertising can help us make decisions about which charities to support, where to volunteer time, or how to interact with the world around us. There is a type of ad called a public service announcement (PSA). According to the Federal Communications Commission (FCC), a PSA is "any announcement (including network) for which no charge is made and which promotes programs, activities, or services of federal, state, or local governments (e.g., recruiting, sale of bonds, etc.) or the programs, activities or services of non-profit organizations (e.g., United Way, Red Cross blood donations, etc.) and other announcements regarded as serving community interests, excluding time signals, routine weather announcements and promotional announcements." PSAs that promote antidrug behaviors, environmental causes, or disease awareness might change the behavior of the audience.

Another way ads help us figure out which tribe we belong to is through celebrity endorsements. When a famous movie star or athlete endorses a product or service or volunteers for a PSA, it can change our behavior. We often do things that our heroes do; so celebrity endorsements help us figure out how to interact with our world.

Ads help us figure out where we belong within society and make decisions about how to spend our money and time.

SMOKEY BEAR

One of the most beloved and long-lasting PSA characters is Smokey Bear. His motto is "Only you can prevent forest fires." In 1940 the federal and state forest services created a postage stamp to let the public know that they could help prevent forest fires. Before Smokey Bear, there were posters that included Death riding through a burning forest or Hitler and several Nazis looking on with glee as U.S. forests burned. Smokey Bear was created in 1944. Since then he has been urging people to be careful with fire in and around the national forests in posters, radio ads, television commercials, and the Internet. He's been featured in coloring books and as a stuffed animal. He is a recognizable cultural icon and remains instrumental in getting the word out to people about how to prevent forest fires.

Smokey Bear warns children and adults of forest fire danger. Here, his image greets people from a highway in Ventura County, California.

WHAT DO YOU THINK?

If you had to sell one thing you own, what would you write in the want ad to get the best price for it?

Suppose that you and a classmate were both selling lemonade for the same price. How would you advertise your lemonade to make it more appealing to customers?

Do you have a favorite ad? What makes it your favorite, and what do you think it says about you?

What is your least favorite ad? What makes you dislike it, and what do you think this says about you?

What do ads aimed at people of your age group say about the group as a whole?

Do you think you have a "tribe"? If so, what does it say about the way you see yourself?

When was the last time you volunteered? What made you volunteer that time, and would you do it again?

How would people know about new goods or services if there were no ads?

Chapter 3

Advertisers are usually clear in their communication of ideas and intent to the consumer. Sometimes, though, a company will put profit above the rights and needs of consumers. Consumers are often at a disadvantage when it comes to advertising. Advertisers have been studying psychology and neuroscience and can target an ad in such a way that the intended customers will feel that they don't and won't fit in until they own the product or use the service.

An example that comes to mind is the Air Jordan shoe craze of the late 1980s. The original high–top basketball Air Jordan Nike® sneakers were expensive and popular. Among some inner-city groups, the desire to fit in and have the same shoes as everyone else, regardless of the consequences, led to violence. A few teens, unable to afford the expensive shoes, stole the shoes from others who had them. These teens committed a crime because they did not want to be the only ones on the neighborhood basketball court without the cool shoes. The ad campaign made the kids want Air Jordans. Without the ad campaign and celebrity endorsement, would kids really fight and even kill over a pair of shoes?

Air Jordan sneakers by Nike on Michael Jordan's feet while playing basketball with the Chicago Bulls. Michael Jordan's affiliation with Nike® in the 1980s sparked a popular fashion trend that resulted in teens fighting over shoes.

The Mind-Body Disconnect

According to the Union of Concerned Scientists, the average person sees around three thousand ads every day in the United States (including web banners, logos, billboards, and commercials). More and more, students see advertising in their schools, where a new trend allows ads in the cafeteria, on the football field, and even in the gym. Teens today influence the buying decisions in a household more than they ever have before, and they spend between $20 and $100 per week on average. Teens alone account for over $1 billion worth of online sales. Advertisers target teens with aggressive ad campaigns that tend to be striking, interactive, and full of teen heartthrob celebrity endorsements. In this age of mobile technology and an increasingly online life, ads are reaching teens through video game tie-ins, movie tie-ins, text messages, and search engine placement.

Unrealistic, "perfect"-bodied Barbie dolls were used to sell fast food to kids.

Advertisers are experts at turning the desire to fit in into the desire to buy. Many of the ads targeting young people prey on the issues that they worry about: fitting in, being attractive to prospective partners, reputation, and feelings of self-worth. Advertising has been called a culprit in such widespread problems as **obesity**, **depression**, and body-dysmorphic disorder (see page 47).

Advertisers may be playing a role in the epidemic of overweight young people in this country. About half the ads kids see on television are for junk food, and it has been documented in several studies that people are more likely to want fast food after seeing a commercial for it.

Advertisers sell everything from clothing to acne medicine to young people. Digitally altered photos of young boys and girls appear in magazine ads. The models are skinnier than they could possibly be in real life, have no wrinkles in their clothes, and are shown with perfectly styled hair and makeup. The clothes they are wearing are trendy, and they've got all the newest gadgets. Images of perfection like this send a message to the unconscious brain: "This is how I should look." A manager at Revlon, Charles Haskell Revson, said, "In the factory we make cosmetics; in the drugstore we sell hope." Consumers hope that the product they buy will help them connect with the image of perfection they desire to achieve.

Shampoo commercials tell consumers that a certain shampoo is better than all the others because it can make hair look and feel perfect. They promise to make your hair look more like the hair on the

When British-based clothing retailer Abercrombie & Fitch became popular in the United States, there was—and still is—much criticism from consumers who felt that the body ideals the retailer advertised were too unrealistic.

model in the commercial. What must be understood is that the model's hair took hours to perfect, with the help of many different stylists. The model may not have even used the specific product being advertised. In fact, there is no way of knowing what other products were used to get the model's hair to look the way it does in the commercial. Some of

DID YOU KNOW?

Many shampoos advertise the importance of the ingredient keratin. What is keratin and why might it be good for the hair? Hair is made up of keratin, which is a protein. How do consumers know whether a shampoo containing the same protein will make their hair longer or stronger, as advertised?

BODY-DYSMORPHIC DISORDER

Body-dysmorphic disorder (BDD) was first diagnosed in 1903 by an Italian psychiatrist named Enrique Morselli. He described seventy-eight of his patients as being "caught by the doubt of deformity" in every waking moment. BDD was not recognized as a disorder until 1987, when it was first included in the Diagnostic and Statistical Manual of Mental Disorders (DSM). People who suffer from BDD are overly concerned about their physical features. Patients with BDD often think they have something wrong with their body. The disease often is diagnosed during the teen years. Those affected spend an obsessive amount of time examining their bodies for disfigurements that are usually only in the mind.

BDD causes many teens to dislike what they see in the mirror.

the images might even have been enhanced using computer graphics. Film and commercial artists can make the special effects disappear in the process; so the viewer is swept up into an artificial world.

Acne commercials are a good example of the use of repetition to sell a product. Advertisers often use a spokesperson, often a celebrity, to tell young viewers that they can control their acne. How many times does a person hear the phrase "your acne"? Will repetition of the

Paging through a magazine, it is hard to remember that models look the way they do after spending hours with professional makeup artists and hair stylists.

phrase convince you that perhaps you do have acne? Teenagers are likely to see a commercial targeted at them several times every day. They will see commercials on TV with a celebrity endorsement. They will see that same campaign in print ads in magazines they read. They will see banners from the same campaign on online sites they traffic. The message preys on the need to be like their peers, and many teens will begin to think that they have a problem with acne. Everyone has a fear that they don't fit in, that they are different. Targeted advertising campaigns use psychology and repetition to cultivate that fear.

The author Peter Nivio Zarlenga used a variation of the quote mentioned earlier from the Revlon executive in one of his novels: "In our factory we make lipstick. In our advertising, we sell hope." Advertising in many ways has trained women and girls to believe in the connection between cosmetics and hope for the future. Teen girls are targeted with cosmetics ads at an unprecedented rate. Reportedly, teenage girls spend over $9 billion per year on skin care products and cosmetics. The industry takes in $50 billion per year and the market steadily grows. Advertisers are especially eager to reach teen girls because it has been shown that people generally stick with the brands they used and liked at an early age. The actress Sharon Gless joked that companies pay top dollar to advertising agencies only if "they get the 18 to 35 age range." Brand

Do you think this girl sees her complexion accurately?

loyalty begins young, and advertisers exploit the hopes and dreams of consumers to capture that loyalty.

Advertisers are using social media as their newest tool. People have the technology to chronicle every movement of their lives. Surfing on the Internet can now be shared through Facebook "likes," Tweets, and Google +1s. Photos can be sent from a phone to the World Wide Web in seconds. A person's life online can either be documented with real photos and constant updates or lived completely through cartoon representations of the person online. There is even a web series, called *The Guild*, that tells the story of a group of nerds in real life, who spend so much time playing an online role-playing game that they have trouble with their lives outside the game.

Advertisers now have both the real world and the virtual world in which to insinuate their brands into the lives and minds of customers. Advertisers on Facebook offer an interactive experience with their audience. The newest advertiser is the Social Media Expert, who cultivates a following online and tries to moderate discussion with, and for, customers. When logging in to a site, each consumer has the responsibility to read the site's privacy policies. Many websites not only track people's browsing habits; they sell the data they collect to advertisers, who use the information to better target their advertising. Advertisers target consumer's preferences,

DID YOU KNOW?

Marketers believe that teens influence family decisions by the sheer fact that they often are the only ones in the family that possess enough knowledge of the Internet to do the research for family products.

Facebook is one of the largest influences in advertising today. Here, CEO and founder of Facebook, Mark Zuckerberg, speaks to advertising partners about how to target their ads using social media.

and now they can gather data about a person's likes and dislikes, keyword searches, click-throughs, and other statistics.

Shockvertisements and Unhealthy Addictions

Beyond preying on people's insecurities, some advertisers are using more and more controversial and disturbing images and ideas to make emotional connections in the minds of ad viewers. **Shockvertisements** use images to deliberately startle or offend the viewer in order to create a desired effect. Many of these deliberately disturbing ads are targeted toward teens to promote awareness of diseases or to deliver PSAs. Ads that push the boundaries have been around for at least twenty years. One of the most popular ads during the late 1980s was the "brain on drugs" PSAs. The ads displayed an egg as the brain and an egg in a frying pan as the brain on drugs. Years later a similar PSA was released with the actress Rachel Leigh Cook. In the second ad, the egg metaphor was taken a little further; Rachel used the pan to smash the egg and then smashed the rest of the kitchen, which represented the drug user's family and friends. There is little conclusive evidence that these ads affect behavior in a positive manner. Some psychiatrists argue that because the ads are shocking, they are more memorable and so become viral trending topics that people talk about for a few weeks.

In 2009 an ad showed a man opening a can and pouring a goopy, fatty mess into a glass. The ad was designed to teach viewers how many calories are in sugary soft drinks and to persuade people to think about switching to seltzer or plain water as a healthier alternative. While it might be interesting to know whether this particular ad had an effect on soda (pop) consumption, drinking soda may not be the real problem. Perhaps we have become a consumption-based society because of the influence of advertising in our lives. Ellen Willis, an American journalist, wrote, "Mass consumption, advertising, and mass art are a corporate Frankenstein; while they reinforce the system, they also undermine it." Mary Shelley's book *Frankenstein* is about a doctor who tries to help society by experimenting with life and death.

His experiment, which produces a monster, symbolizes the complexity in the world and the thin line between good and evil. So is soda the "bad" thing? Or is the consumer's emotional tie and addiction to soda the problem? Another question to consider is whether we as a society would consume so much sugary soda if we weren't conditioned to want it from watching the thousands of ads we see every year.

McDonald's and Burger King, sellers of fast, cheap food, are part of a $110–billion industry in the United States alone. Fast-food chains need consumers as much as consumers addicted to fast food need the chains. Recent green and "real food" campaigns have criticized fast food for helping to make Americans fat and unhealthy. Americans have been binge eating at fast-food chains for over sixty years.

While a McDonald's Egg McMuffin might have only 300 calories, it has 87 percent of the daily recommended allowance of cholesterol. High levels of cholesterol can be associated with heart disease.

Before recent regulation, there was no way to know the caloric content of fast-food items. People had no idea what ingredients were in the burgers and fries they were eating, including all the unhealthy trans fats and processed foodstuffs. Today fast-food chains must publish the nutrition information of all their menu items; this information is often also found online. Movie tie-in marketing and marketing geared toward children ten and under make fast-food chains one of the more dangerous advertisers. Fast food may be considered fine in moderation, but when children are constantly bombarded with the images and the subtle manipulations of fast-food commercials, it is hard for parents and kids not to want more and more and more.

During the late twentieth century, tobacco and alcohol companies targeted teens for their products even though it was illegal for teens to purchase cigarettes and alcohol. Studies found that the Philip Morris company (known for the Marlboro Man) targeted ads to kids as young as thirteen. Public outrage and complaints from consumers weren't enough to stop the advertisers from trying to get younger and younger customers. The earlier people start smoking, the longer they will be buying cigarettes, the more cigarettes will become part of their identity.

Joe Camel, the cartoon mascot for Camel brand cigarettes, was first seen in print advertising in the United States in 1987. Just four years after Joe Camel's appearance in ads, as many six-year-old children were able to identify the Joe Camel mascot with cigarettes as could identify Mickey Mouse with Disney. It has been proved that tobacco companies knew that smoking causes cancer long before the U.S. government forced them to add warning labels on the packaging. Camel denied that Joe Camel ads were directed at kids.

In 1991 Janet Mangini, an attorney in San Francisco, sued R. J. Reynolds (the company that owns the Camel brand). Her evidence suggested that, regardless of the intended target of the ad campaign, teen smoking had increased dramatically in the four years since the campaign had started. Mangini said that income from sales of Camel brand cigarettes to teens in 1988 was $6 million and that in 1992 it was $476 million. In the end, R. J. Reynolds was forced to pay $10 million toward an antismoking campaign targeting teens and to abandon the Joe Camel mascot.

Critics of advertising argued that an ad campaign that tried to make a cancer-causing product attractive to children was something that went too far. They pointed to some remarks of Pope John Paul II: "Young people are threatened . . . by the evil use of advertising techniques that stimulate the natural inclination to avoid hard work by promising the immediate satisfaction of every desire." Recent regulations have cracked down a bit on the use of misleading and obscure terms on food packaging but have not been able to do the same for other industries where the use of deliberately false or misleading facts, images, or statements to persuade people to buy a service or prod-

David Kessler (Food and Drug Administration Commissioner) and Donna Shalala (Health and Human Services Secretary) hold up a Camel brand cigarette ad with the character Joe Camel, who appealed to kids.

uct continues to be widespread. For example, at one point companies used the word *light* or *lite* to describe a product, the implication being that the food had fewer calories than similar products; often, however, the word didn't refer to anything.

Some natural cosmetics and skin care companies use the phrase "chemical-free" to imply that they only use natural ingredients. The phrase chemical-free may not actually mean anything, however, given that everything on earth is made up of chemicals. There is nothing that is chemical-free. So what does chemical-free mean when a company advertises a product as such? How is a consumer to know?

Ads Aimed at YOU

Sometimes ads use language that affects the listener in a more personal way. An ad using the pronoun "you" speaks directly to the consumer. Advertisers study what shows their target audience watches, what fears their target audience has, and what celebrities their target audience follows. Advertisers are able to track the target audience's behavior online to see what websites have been browsed. When a person sees an online ad, it is likely aimed directly at him or her. Advertisers have learned how to play on the viewer's desires and fears, knowledge about the world, and unconscious thoughts.

Targeted ads will try to convince consumers that they want things they may not have wanted before they saw the ad. In the early 2000s a pharmaceutical company targeted music-loving teens for an acne product by promising free music for visiting the website and signing up for a free trial. These ads were placed on websites about music, on MTV, and on other music-related media.

The prescription acne medication Differin, produced by a company called Galderma, brought an audience to its website with the lure of free music and then presented the responders with ads about acne and the company's acne medicine in an attempt to make the customers think that they might have a problem and need a prescription for its product to make it better. Teens were required to download a coupon from a website and go to a doctor before the acne medicine ever made it into their hands. It turned out to be a successful marketing campaign. A study found that the teens who went to the website just for the free music were more likely to request acne medicine the next time they saw their family physician than those who hadn't been to the website.

Many companies offer free products for "liking" them on Facebook or following them on Twitter. Once you like or follow a company, the company has access to some or all of your online data (depending on privacy settings). Free gear means a little upfront cost for the company for a long-term benefit of returning customers.

By luring people to "like" their Facebook page with contests, Wendy's advertisers hope to be able to target ad campaigns directly to consumers through social media.

CIGARETTES AND NICOTINE

Cigarette smoking is the cause of many preventable diseases. Many cigarette smokers are unable to quit smoking because of a nicotine addiction. The drug causes a sense of well-being called euphoria, which reinforces the addiction to smoking. Nicotine affects both mood and performance and is one of the more readily available addictive drugs.

That was one of the cigarette manufacturers' tactics when they were targeting teens and young adults during the 1980s. They would offer free merchandise with the points collected from cigarette packs and cartons. Kids smoked more so that they could collect points to "buy" a leather jacket, for instance. They didn't realize that the money they spent on the cigarettes to get the points could have bought two or three leather jackets. It was the lure of something "free." The American film producer Joseph E. Levine famously said, "You can fool all the people all the time if the advertising is right and the budget is big enough."

Today the cost is often a loss of privacy. To get free information or free stuff or a chance to win something, consumers often give up their personal information. Companies then turn around and use the data they've collected to better aim ads at the audience they want. Knowing more about the audience allows them to sell the products more effectively.

Privacy and the Internet

How do companies invade privacy? In this age, companies track people's movement online using click-through statistics, cookies, and other online tools. Each click on a path becomes part of a vast statistical analysis that is then used to plan the next marketing campaign. In addition, information from pop-up ads, banners ads on commercial websites, and data from the Global Positioning System (GPS) is being collected from millions of people every day. The information is then put into vast databases.

When a reader of fashion blogs clicks through several different sites, the ads on the sites being visited begin to be tailored to fashion. Once that person clicks through to a fashion sales site and makes an order, the ads change to indicate that the site wants you to come back. If instead the reader searches a particular band using a search engine, the iTunes ads will suddenly have that band's logo or most recent album as the centerpiece. The only way to stop this kind of data collection from happening is to clear your computer's browser cache frequently. Otherwise advertisers can track your movements electronically. A person doesn't even have to be involved. Online services have built sophisticated programs to automatically track you and target ads to you.

There have been studies that claim to be able to take anonymous Twitter or blog accounts and determine gender solely on the basis of the language usage in the posts. Data from purchases can be mined and studied for patterns by advertising agencies to target ads. There is no escape. Even when a person uses cash to buy a product, marketers now use the "frequent buyer card" to collect the data. Many stores offer this kind of card, including grocery stores, bookstores, and pet stores. These cards collect data about what is purchased using the card. At grocery stores what is purchased with the card will influence which coupons are printed on the receipt. Data from the people who shop in a store is used to determine discounts, regular pricing, and even what new products to stock. Every purchase, every interest, can be traced and used to target your "user experience."

Advertisers use rewards cards to track the buying habits and purchases of consumers in order to better target ads and increase sales.

Consumers Are a Part of the Ad

Not only do the advertisers track millions of pieces of information about customers, consumers are now a part of the brand experience. The message has become the **interface**; the point of connection between the consumer and the brand is now seamless. Consumers are even asked to participate in ad campaigns. For example, recently there was a vote for the new Old Spice Guy. The campaign took place entirely on the Internet. The ad campaign was new and different. Ads were put on YouTube and spread via reblogging and social media. Fans interacted with the two candidates and could then vote for the brand's new spokesman.

For over thirty years off and on during the mid–1900s,

DID YOU KNOW?

Soda sales have been declining since 2005. Even in decline, 9.4 billion cases of soda were sold in 2009—an average of two cans of soda daily for every person in the United States.

61

there was a "cola war" going on. Pepsi® and Coke® were competing for customers through commercials and in the aisles of stores to see which would be the top-selling cola brand. Coca-Cola®, the first cola to enter the scene, was trademarked in 1893. Pepsi started in 1898, but the company officially opened its doors in 1965. So the advertisers created the idea of Pepsi as the cola for a new generation: the "Pepsi generation." Ads told consumers that in a blind taste test, people preferred Pepsi to Coke.

Today companies have an online presence. They want consumers to follow and like them in different online communities. Companies need consumers to talk to each other about their products. Amazon.com was one of the first websites to build an interface for its customers to review products. The idea caught on, and now there is rarely a commercial website that doesn't ask customers to comment on products. Who is more trustworthy—the average customer or the company that makes the product? Blogging about products has become a new industry. Companies even give popular bloggers free products in the hopes that they will review the product on their site and grab a few more customers through word of mouth.

WHAT DO YOU THINK?

Do you think a manufacturer has a responsibility to provide truthful information in advertisements?

How many ads do you think you see every day, and where do you see them?

Are there ads in your school? Do you think it makes a difference if there are ads in school or not?

Are there things that you want that you don't need? Do you think advertising made you want these things?

What do you think someone studying your online movements would conclude about you? Does it make you uncomfortable to imagine someone using your web-surfing habits to create advertisements geared directly to you?

Chapter 4

Advertisements seep into every facet of modern life. Ads drive our economy. Without ads people wouldn't know where to get the goods and services they need. Without ads people wouldn't learn about new research, new products, or new services. Without ads researchers wouldn't be able to let people know about their results. Without ads patients wouldn't be able to find doctors, and employers wouldn't be able to find job seekers. Yet even with all the benefits ads provide, there are costs. Ads target emotions, not logic. Decision-making based strictly on emotions doesn't always lead us in the right direction.

The American author William Feather wrote, "The philosophy behind much advertising is based on the old observation that every man is really two men—the man he is and the man he wants to be." Individuals must find a balance between who they are and who they want to be. Advertising is designed to tell consumers who they want to be.

Fashion designer Yves Saint-Laurent once said, "The most beautiful makeup of a woman is passion. But cosmetics are easier to buy." These young women shop for cosmetics in a superstore that targets them for increased sales.

The Joe Camel controversy in the early 1990s taught advertisers a valuable lesson in ethics. Regardless of the intention of the advertisers, the result was that more teens were smoking after Joe Camel appeared in ads than before. This and similar cases brought to the public eye the need to regulate advertisements in order to protect consumers and manufacturers alike.

Regulation

Advertising is essential for the economy to keep moving forward. The Federal Communications Commission (FCC) and the Federal Trade Commission (FTC) work in many ways to help protect consumers from unscrupulous advertising. They also work to protect companies from unfair practices.

The FTC is the governmental department that protects the consumer. For instance, in 2007 the FTC created the National Do Not Call Registry. The registry allows all consumers to opt out of receiving calls from telemarketers, who call home and work phone numbers with a sales pitch. Before 2007 there was no option to get a name removed from the lists of telemarketers. Telemarketers are taught to use aggressive tactics to make it hard for people to say no. The FTC also protects consumers through enforcement of the U.S. truth-in-advertising laws and guidelines. Strict rules determine what can be considered unscrupulous in an ad. When an advertiser is found guilty of breaking the truth-in-advertising laws, the company can be fined.

Congress enacted the Telephone Consumer Protection Act (TCPA) in 1991 in an effort to address the number of telephone marketing calls. Should similar laws be made to protect people from unwanted text messages, e-mails, or online banner ads?

The FCC regulates the media. It is responsible for enforcing the laws and guidelines of broadcast communications. As technology changes, the FCC reacts to the changes and updates the guidelines.

"Advertising has learned to tell the truth attractively about products. When the product is good, and the truth is told, we have the appealing combination that secures sales and keeps the wheels of industry turning." This comment was written by an American author and minister.

Since the consumer is the key part of the advertising industry, it actually hurts the industry when customers lose faith in products or services. In 1971 the major trade associates formed an alliance called the National Advertising Review Council. This council has two organizations that investigate claims of abuse or misrepresentation: the National Advertising Division (NAD) and the Children's Advertising Review Unit

In an age when childhood obesity is at an all-time high, all these unhealthy foods are marketed directly to kids using animation characters, fun colors, and cool prizes. Here, Senator Tom Harkin, a Democrat from Iowa, displays just a few examples of this type of targeted marketing.

(CARU). By policing itself, the advertising industry can stop glaring violations of laws from getting into the governmental court system. If the industry polices itself, the government will not have to create new laws to further regulate the system.

Consumers must also take part in the regulation process. If something seems too good to be true, or malicious or harmful, customers have many options for reporting their concern. For instance, a customer who feels that an ad for an acne medication has misrepresented the product can file a claim with the Food and Drug Administration (FDA), which oversees laws relating to drugs. Claims can also be made through local Better Business Bureau offices or online.

While people may argue about the benefits of advertising, it isn't going anywhere. Advertising is too entwined in our economy and our way of life. Some would argue that government regulation should be stricter, while others believe that the industry itself is a better policing agent than the government. Both sides would agree that the consumer also has a responsibility to report any abuses seen.

Advertising and Society

Advertising has driven changes within society and is so tied to it that the debate on its benefits is overshadowed by just how large and complex the industry is. Advertising drives competition and innovation, and it reflects cultural norms and helps individuals establish identity within society. It also performs a much needed basic function of connecting goods and services with consumers. However, there have been and continue to be many detrimental costs to advertising. Many books and hundreds of articles deal with body image and its relationship to advertising.

As society moves toward a more integrated advertising module, we should remember some important points. First, advertising reflects our cultural values. When we participate in marketing campaigns with the use of technology, we as consumers should try to think more critically about the product and company. We should consider what our participation in the campaigns reveals about our values to our friends and neighbors. When we participate in ads, we must remember that the goal of the advertisement is to make money. So any emotional connection with the brand should be scrutinized.

Consumers no longer passively view or listen to ads. Increasingly they interact with advertisers mostly through online social media. They have power to influence the brands through that interaction.

WHAT DO YOU THINK?

Do you think the benefits outweigh the negative aspects of advertising? Why or why not?

Do you think of yourself as a wise consumer? Why or why not?

Do you think it is easy to tell when advertisers make false claims?

What do you think should be done about false advertising?

Timeline

Advertising in the United States

1704 – The first want ad is placed in the *Boston News-Letter*.

1843 – Volney Palmer opens the first advertising agency in the world.

1893 – Coca-Cola is trademarked.

1902 – Pepsi-Cola is trademarked.

1906 – Passage of the Pure Food and Drugs Act.

1914 – The Federal Trade Commission is started.

1925 – The Better Business Bureau is created.

1929 – The Great Depression begins; advertising spending drops by over $1.5 billion.

1930 – *Advertising Age* becomes the first magazine for advertising professionals.

1942 – The War Advisory Council is created with a $350-million budget to spend on World War II–related PSAs.

1953 – The Advertising Research Foundation is founded.

1955 – The Marlboro Man ad campaign kicks off.

1958 – The National Association of Broadcasters bans broadcasting of subliminal ads.

1964 – The *New Yorker* and other magazines ban cigarette ads after the U.S. Surgeon General declares them to be "hazardous to health."

1971 – Congress passes a law prohibiting cigarette commercials from being broadcast on TV.

1971 – The National Advertising Review Council is established.

1976 – Advertisements are granted protection under the First Amendment.

1981 – MTV begins broadcasting. Advertisers respond by producing commercials targeted to its youthful audience.

1993 – Around 5 million people are using the Internet/World Wide Web (2.3 percent of the U.S. population).

1998 – Cigarette companies agree to curb advertisements and pay some medical fees.

1999 – Internet advertising reaches $2 billion, with 36.6 percent of the U.S. population getting online.

2006 – A $90-million settlement is reached between Google Inc. and advertisers who claimed they were billed incorrectly for clicks on banner ads.

2009 – Internet use reaches 78 percent of the U.S. population.

2011 – Morgan Spurlock's documentary *POM Wonderful Presents: The Greatest Movie Ever Sold*, about advertising in the lives of Americans, is released.

2013 – Over 70 percent of all mobile phone users have smartphones.

Glossary

anthropologist—A person who studies human cultures and societies.

banner—An advertisement graphic that runs on a World Wide Web page, usually in a rectangle on the top of the page or in the right or left column.

billboard—Usually outdoors, an oversized sign used to display advertisements.

brand—A company or product, often indicated by a service mark or trademark.

branding—The process of using design, slogans, and logos to connect goods or services in the minds of consumers.

campaign—In advertising, a planned course of action to announce and promote a product or service.

classified ad—Communication online, in a printed newspaper or magazine, or on a notice board that advertises goods or services available or wanted.

client—A person or organization using the services of a professional person or company.

commission—Salary or payment for sales made or for work done.

consumer—Any person or group of people that uses a product or service.

copywriter—A person who writes text for advertisements or publicity materials.

cottage industry—Business or manufacturing done in or from the home.

depression—A mental disorder that causes feelings of hopelessness and loneliness, lack of interest, and an inability to concentrate.

economist—A person who studies the production, consumption, and distribution of wealth (money).

endorsement—The act of giving approval or support for a product or service.

gramophone—The name given to the early form of the phonograph, or record player.

ideal—An idea of perfection or excellence.

Industrial Revolution—The period in the late eighteenth and early nineteenth centuries marked by rapid technological development and by the concentration of industry in large establishments and regions.

interface—A place, virtual or physical, where two things (for example systems, people, organizations) meet and interact.

logo—An image or text with design used by an organization to identify a product or a service.

marketing—The act or practice of using advertisements to sell goods or services.

medium—One of various outlets of mass communication—collectively called the media—including television, radio, film, print and online newspapers and magazines, and even circulars and posters.

mores—The moral and ethical beliefs of a particular group that are generally accepted without controversy.

obesity—A medical condition caused by too much fat in the body.

psychologist—A person who studies the mind and behavior in different situations.

publicity—The attention given to a person, product, or service to promote sales or awareness.

shockvertisement—An advertisement that is designed to be surprising, disgusting, or offensive to the audience.

slogan—A motto or phrase used in advertising to identify a product or a service; also known as a tagline.

target—A person or group selected as the mark of an advertising campaign.

trailer—A promotional preview for a movie, which typically includes brief excerpts and insistent use of catchphrases and other publicity devices.

Find Out More

Books

Fletcher, Winston. *Advertising: A Very Short Introduction.* New York: Oxford University Press, 2010.

Lindstrom, Martin. *Brandwashed: Tricks Companies Use to Manipulate Our Minds and Persuade Us to Buy.* New York: Crown Business, 2011.

Metz, Adam. *The Social Customer: How Brands Can Use Social CRM to Acquire, Monetize, and Retain Fans, Friends, and Followers.* New York: McGraw Hill, 2012.

Pincas, Stephane, and Marc Loiseau. *A History of Advertising.* Los Angeles: Taschen, 2008.

Sedivy, Julie. *Sold on Language: How Advertisers Talk to You and What This Says about You.* Malden, MA: Wiley-Blackwell, 2011.

Tungate, Mark. *Adland: A Global History of Advertising.* Philadelphia: Kogan Page, 2007.

Websites

Action Coalition for Media Education
www.acmecoalition.org

Adbusters
www.adbusters.org

Advertising Research Foundation
www.thearf.org

Better Business Bureau

www.bbb.org

Common Sense Media

www.commonsensemedia.org

Federal Trade Commission

www.ftc.gov

Media Education Foundation

www.mediaed.org

National Association of Broadcasters

www.nab.org

United States Food and Drug Administration

www.fda.gov

Videos

Dove Evolution

www.youtube.com/watch?v=iYhCn0jf46U

Index

Page numbers in boldface are illustrations.

About the Author

Aubrey Hicks received a bachelor's degree in English from Moravian College and a master's degree in Library and Information Science from the University of Illinois at Urbana-Champaign. She has worked as a reference librarian and in academic and publishing administration. Currently, Ms. Hicks is an assistant director for a university research center on governance. Ms. Hicks loves reading anything with words.